The Quote Book

Gems from the pen of Ellen G. White

Key to Abbreviations

AA	*The Acts of the Apostles*	SD	*Sons and Daughters of God*
AH	*The Adventist Home*	1SM	*Selected Messages,* book 1, etc.
1BC	*The SDA Bible Commentary,* vol. 1, etc.	ST	*Signs of the Times*
CG	*Child Guidance*	1T	*Testimonies,* vol. 1, etc.
COL	*Christ's Object Lessons*	TDG	*This Day With God*
CPT	*Counsels to Parents and Teachers*	TM	*Testimonies to Ministers*
CS	*Counsels on Stewardship*	TMK	*"That I May Know Him"*
DA	*The Desire of Ages*	UL	*The Upward Look*
EW	*Early Writings*		
GC	*The Great Controversy*		
GW	*Gospel Workers*		
IHP	*In Heavenly Places*		
LS	*Life Sketches*		
Mar	*Maranatha*		
MB	*Thoughts From the Mount of Blessing*		
MH	*The Ministry of Healing*		
MLT	*My Life Today*		
MYP	*Messages to Young People*		
OHC	*Our High Calling*		
PP	*Patriarchs and Prophets*		
PK	*Prophets and Kings*		
RH	*Review and Herald*		
SC	*Steps to Christ*		

The Quote Book

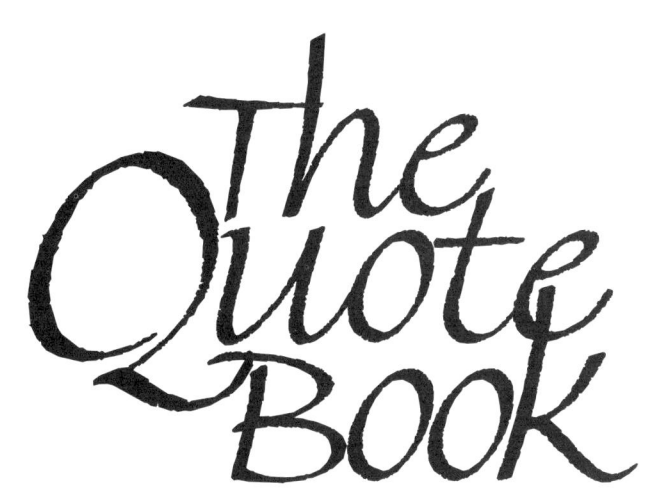

Gems from the pen of Ellen G. White
Compiled by Phyllis C. Bailey

Review and Herald® Publishing Association
Hagerstown, MD 21740

Copyright © 1994 by
Review and Herald® Publishing Association

The author assumes full responsibility for the accuracy of all facts and quotations as cited in this book.

This book was
Edited by Penny Estes Wheeler
Designed by Patricia S. Wegh
Cover design by Helcio Deslandes
Typeset 18/20 Garamond

PRINTED IN U.S.A.

98 97 96   10 9 8 7 6 5 4 3 2

Library of Congress Cataloging in Publication Data
White, Ellen Gould Harmon, 1827-1915.
   The quote book: 316 gems from the pen of Ellen White / Ellen G. White ; compiled by Phyllis C. Bailey.
       p.   cm.
   1. Christian life—Seventh-day Adventist authors.   I. Bailey, Phyllis C.   II. Title.
BX6111.W514   1994
248.4'86732—dc20
                                                                94-27763
                                                                   CIP

ISBN 0-8280-0863-9

By the side of every soul is an angel presence. TDG 332.

For he shall give his angels charge over thee, to keep thee in all thy ways. Ps. 91:11.

The outside appearance is an index to the heart. 1T 136.

Ye are . . . known and read of all men. 2 Cor. 3:2.

The Quote Book

We may ask of God great things and He will give them us. TDG 60.

Call unto me, and I will answer thee, and shew thee great and mighty things, which thou knowest not. Jer. 33:3.

All things are possible to those that believe. IHP 81.

All things, whatsoever ye shall ask in prayer, believing, ye shall receive. Matt. 21:22.

It is not enough to believe *about* Christ; we must believe *in* Him.
DA 347.

Believe *in* the Lord your God, so shall ye be established. 2 Chron. 20:20.

The Quote Book

Having done the best we can, then we are to leave all results with God. TM 184.

And whatsoever ye do, do it heartily, as to the Lord. Col. 3:23.

The Lord will help all who will do all their best, walking humbly with God. IHP 278.

Now unto him that is able to do exceeding abundantly above all that we ask or think, according to the power that worketh in us. Eph. 3:20.

Many who are qualified to do excellent work accomplish little because they attempt little. MH 498.

Ye shall rejoice in all that ye put your hand unto. Deut. 12:7.

Remember that what is worth doing at all is worth doing well.
MLT 219.

Whatsoever thy hand findeth to do, do it with thy might.
Eccl. 9:10.

The Quote Book

The Bible was given for practical purposes. 1SM 20.

And now, brethren, I commend you to God, and to the word of his grace, which is able to build you up. Acts 20;32.

A familiarity with the Word of God is our only hope. 1SM 228.

My people are destroyed for lack of knowledge. Hosea 4:6.

The Quote Book

Prayer is the breath of the soul, the channel of all blessings.
Mar 85.

Delight thyself also in the Lord; and he shall give thee the desires of thine heart. Ps. 37:4.

Let us not make ourselves miserable over tomorrow's burdens. IHP 269.

Casting all your care upon him; for he careth for you.
1 Peter 5:7.

True character is not something shaped from without, or put on, but it is something radiating from within.
TDG 146.

And thus are the secrets of his heart made manifest. 1 Cor. 14:25.

Character is the great harvest of life. MB 90.

But he knoweth the way that I take: when he hath tried me, I shall come forth as gold. Job 23:10.

꙳ The Quote Book ꙳

The more closely we discern Jesus, the more clearly we shall see our own defects of character. TDG 89.

Look unto me, and be ye saved. Isa. 45:22.

We should encourage a cheerful, hopeful, peaceful frame of mind; for our health depends upon our so doing. MLT 151.

A merry heart doeth good like a medicine. Prov. 17:22.

Christians should be the most cheerful and happy people that live. MLT 177.

Whoso trusteth in the Lord, happy is he. Prov. 16:20.

The education and training of their children to be Christians is the highest service that parents can render to God.
COL 195.

I have no greater joy than to hear that my children walk in truth.
3 John 4.

The Quote Book

Make Christ first and last and best in everything. 7T 46.

I will rejoice in the Lord, I will joy in the God of my salvation. Hab. 3:18.

What food is to the body, Christ must be to the soul. DA 389.

Taste and see that the Lord is good: blessed is the man that trusteth in him. Ps. 34:8.

≪ The Quote Book ≫

To be half a Christian and half a worldly man makes you about one-hundredth part a Christian and all the rest worldly. 2T 264.

No man can serve two masters: for either he will hate the one, and love the other; or else he will hold to the one, and despise the other. Matt. 6:24.

Everything that Christians do should be as transparent as the sunlight. MB 68.

Be thou an example of the believers, in word, in conversation. 1 Tim. 4:12.

Christians are Christ's jewels, bought with an infinite price.
UL 372.

And they shall be mine, saith the Lord of hosts, in that day when I make up my jewels. Mal. 3:17.

A kind, courteous Christian is the most powerful argument that can be produced in favor of Christianity. GW 122.

Be kindly affectioned one to another with brotherly love; in honour preferring one another. Rom. 12:10.

The more we study the life of Christ with a heart to learn, the more Christlike we become.
TMK 118.

But we all, with open face beholding as in a glass the glory of the Lord, are changed into the same image. 2 Cor. 3:18.

Nothing else in this world is so dear to God as His church. Nothing is guarded by Him with such jealous care. 6T 42.

Feed the church of God, which he hath purchased with his own blood. Acts 20:28.

The world will be convinced, not by what the pulpit teaches, but by what the church lives. 7T 16.

Let your light so shine before men, that they may see your good works. Matt. 5:16.

Every chapter and every verse of the Bible is a communication from God to men. PP 504.

All scripture is given by inspiration of God. 2 Tim. 3:16.

Communion with God encourages good thoughts, noble aspirations, clear perceptions of truth, and lofty purposes of action. MYP 431.

It is good for me to draw near to God. Ps. 73:28.

Every sin acknowledged before God with a contrite heart, He will remove. TM 93.

Whosoever believeth in him shall receive remission of sins. Acts 10:43.

Consecrate yourself to God in the morning; make this your very first work. SC 70.

Consecrate yourselves to day to the Lord. Ex. 32:29.

The Quote Book

It would be well for us to spend a thoughtful hour each day in contemplation of the life of Christ. DA 83.

I determined not to know any thing among you, save Jesus Christ. 1 Cor. 2:2.

He who is truly converted will be so filled with the love of God that he will long to impart to others the joy that he himself possesses. 9T 30.

Ye should shew forth the praises of him who hath called you out of darkness into his marvellous light. 1 Peter 2:9.

Decisions may be made in a moment that fix one's condition forever. 2SM 165.

Behold, I set before you the way of life, and the way of death. Jer. 21:8.

Eternal life is worth everything to us or it is worth nothing. OHC 94.

What is a man profited, if he shall gain the whole world, and lose his own soul? Matt. 16:26.

A right example will do more to benefit the world than all our profession. COL 383.

In all things shewing thyself a pattern of good works.
Titus 2:7.

Those who are close students of the Word, following Christ in humility of soul, will not go to extremes. GW 317.

Be not righteous over much; neither make thyself over wise. Eccl. 7:16.

We have nothing to fear for the future, except as we shall forget the way the Lord has led us, and His teaching in our past history. LS 196.

Thou shalt remember all the ways which the Lord thy God led thee. Deut. 8:2.

The Quote Book

A strong, helpful grasp of the hand of a true friend is worth more than gold and silver.
TDG 144.

Love is strong as death. . . . Many waters cannot quench love.
S. of Sol. 8:6, 7.

The warmth of true friendship, the love that binds heart to heart, is a foretaste of the joys of heaven. MH 360.

A friend loveth at all times. Prov. 17:17.

🌱 *The Quote Book* 🍃

It is through the gift of Christ that we receive every blessing. 8T 287, 288.

Every good gift and every perfect gift is from above. James 1:17.

You cannot give to God anything that He has not first given you. MYP 407.

Thou shalt give unto the Lord thy God, according as the Lord thy God hath blessed thee. Deut. 16:10.

The Lord never requires His people to offer more than they are able, but according to their ability. 5T 269.

Every man shall give as he is able, according to the blessing of the Lord. Deut. 16:17.

There are only two places in the universe where we can deposit our treasures—in God's storehouse or in Satan's. TDG 303.

Ye cannot serve God and mammon. Matt. 6:24.

The more men learn of God, the greater will be their admiration of His character. GC 678.

Acquaint now thyself with him, and be at peace. Job 22:21.

The Lord is not far from the soul who seeks Him. TDG 232.

Draw nigh to God, and he will draw nigh to you. James 4:8.

In the expenditure of money, in the use of time, strength, opportunities, let every Christian look to God for guidance.
MH 208.

For this God is our God for ever and ever: he will be our guide even unto death. Ps. 48:14.

The love of God cannot remain in our possession unless it is expressed. UL 361.

If a man love me, he will keep my words: and my Father will love him. John 14:23.

If we thought and talked more of Jesus, and less of self, we should have far more of His presence. IHP 92.

Then they that feared the Lord spake often one to another: and the Lord hearkened, and heard it. Mal. 3:16.

The Quote Book

Bad habits are more easily formed than good ones and are given up with more difficulty. CG 202.

For that which I do I allow not: for what I would, that do I not; but what I hate, that do I. Rom. 7:15.

Those who in everything make God first and last and best are the happiest people in the world. MLT 161.

My soul shall be joyful in the Lord. Ps. 35:9.

Seeking the good of others is the way in which true happiness can be found. CS 24.

He that hath mercy on the poor, happy is he. Prov. 14:21.

Our happiness comes not from what is around us, but from what is within us; not from what we have, but from what we are. MLT 185.

I have learned, in whatsoever state I am, therewith to be content. Phil. 4:11.

A person whose mind is quiet and satisfied in God is in the pathway to health. MLT 150.

To be spiritually minded is life and peace. Rom. 8:6.

A heart of faith and love is dearer to God than the most costly gift. DA 615.

Blessed are the pure in heart: for they shall see God. Matt. 5:8.

If we reach heaven at last, our heaven must begin here below. TDG 122.

Seek those things which are above. Col. 3:1.

The Quote Book

When God sees us doing all we can on our part, then He will help us. 1T 663.

God is able to make all grace abound toward you; that ye, always having all sufficiency in all things, may abound to every good work. 2 Cor. 9:8.

He who gives to the needy blesses others and is blessed himself in a still greater degree. 9T 253.

The merciful man doeth good to his own soul. Prov. 11:17.

There must be a power working from within, a new life from above, before men can be changed from sin to holiness. SC 18.

I will put my spirit within you, and cause you to walk in my statutes. Eze. 36:27.

You cannot be kind, true, courteous, unselfish, without the Holy Spirit's help. TDG 288.

But we all . . . are changed into the same image from glory to glory even as by the Spirit of the Lord. 2 Cor. 3:18.

God can teach you more in one moment by His Holy Spirit than you could learn from the great men of the earth. Mar 23.

But the Comforter, which is the Holy Ghost, whom the Father will send in my name, he shall teach you all things. John 14:26.

Those who are Christians in the home will be Christians in the world. MLT 102.

Learn first to shew piety at home. 1 Tim. 5:4.

What a man *is* has a greater influence than what he *says*. TDG 146.

The hidden man of the heart . . . is in the sight of God of great price. 1 Peter 3:4.

Honor, integrity, and truth must be preserved at any cost to self. GW 447.

What doth the Lord require of thee, but to do justly? Micah 6:8.

Those who abide in Jesus will be happy, cheerful, and joyful in God. MYP 431.

Let them . . . that love thy name be joyful in thee. Ps. 5:11.

Christ was treated as we deserve, that we might be treated as He deserves. DA 25.

For he hath made him to be sin for us, who knew no sin; that we might be made the righteousness of God in him. 2 Cor. 5:21.

By the lives of Christ's followers the world will judge the Saviour. TDG 353.

They may by your good works, which they shall behold, glorify God. 1 Peter 2:12.

Words of kindness are as welcome as the smile of angels.
MH 158.

**A word fitly spoken is like apples of gold in pictures of silver.
Prov. 25:11.**

Our words and actions constitute the fruit we bear. A consecrated life is a daily, living sermon. 4T 609.

The brethren came and testified of the truth that is in thee. 3 John 3.

The Word of God contains our life insurance policy. UL 78.

He that heareth my word . . . hath everlasting life. John 5:24.

The Quote Book

It is the little things in life that reveal a person's real character.
OHC 227.

**Thou good servant: . . . thou hast been faithful in a very little.
Luke 19:17.**

He who loves Christ the most will do the greatest amount of good. DA 250.

But if any man love God, the same is known of him. 1 Cor. 8:3.

We should love and respect one another, notwithstanding the faults and imperfections that we cannot help seeing. SC 121.

With all lowliness and meekness, with longsuffering, forbearing one another in love. Eph. 4:2.

Man's necessity is God's opportunity. 1T 230.

Jesus . . . said unto them, With men this is impossible; but with God all things are possible. Matt. 19:26.

To gain a proper understanding of the marriage relation is the work of a lifetime. 7T 45.

Live joyfully with the wife whom thou lovest all the days of the life . . . which he hath given thee. Eccl. 9:9.

God will do marvelous things for those who trust in Him. 4T 163.

Blessed are all they that put their trust in him. Ps. 2:12.

The world is not so much in need of great minds, as of good men, who are a blessing in their homes. GW 204.

The glory of children are their fathers. Prov. 17:6.

The way to the throne of mercy is always open. TDG 199.

Let us therefore come boldly unto the throne of grace, that we may obtain mercy, and find grace to help in time of need. Heb. 4:16.

A contented mind, a cheerful spirit, is health to the body and strength to the soul. 1T 702.

Godliness with contentment is great gain. 1 Tim. 6:6.

The king upon his throne has no higher work than has the mother. AH 231.

A woman that feareth the Lord, she shall be praised. Prov. 31:30.

The gates are open for every mother who would lay her burdens at the Saviour's feet.
DA 512.

Come unto me, all ye that labour and are heavy laden, and I will give you rest. Matt. 11:28.

"Looking unto Jesus" is ever to be our motto. 7T 94.

Let us run with patience the race that is set before us, looking unto Jesus the author and finisher of our faith. Heb. 12:1, 2.

Satan trembles and flees before the weakest soul who finds refuge in [the Lord's] mighty name. DA 131.

Submit yourselves therefore to God. Resist the devil, and he will flee from you. James 4:7.

Do not neglect secret prayer, for it is the soul of religion. 1T 163.

Pray without ceasing. 1 Thess. 5:17.

Our neighbor is every one who is the property of God.
COL 376.

Thou shalt love thy neighbor as thyself. Lev. 19:18.

Many have such a constant care for themselves that they give God no opportunity to care for them. 2T 657.

They all look to their own way, every one for his gain. Isa. 56:11.

At every stage of development our life may be perfect; yet if God's purpose for us is fulfilled, there will be continual advancement. COL 65.

The path of the just is as the shining light, that shineth more and more unto the perfect day. Prov. 4:18.

It is not returning to the Lord His own that makes men poor; withholding tends to poverty. CS 36.

He which soweth sparingly shall reap also sparingly. 2 Cor. 9:6.

The poor should be treated with as much interest and attention as the rich. 4T 551.

Be of the same mind one toward another. Rom. 12:16.

The firmer hold we have on heaven, the greater will be our power for usefulness. IHP 312.

God is my strength and power. 2 Sam. 22:33.

All who consecrate soul, body, and spirit to God will be constantly receiving a new endowment of physical and mental power. DA 827.

As many as received him, to them gave he power. John 1:12.

From a worldly point of view, money is power; but from the Christian standpoint, love is power. 4T 138.

Love . . . and your reward shall be great. Luke 6:35.

Nothing tends more to promote health of body and of soul than does a spirit of gratitude and praise. MH 251.

Sing praises unto his name; for it is pleasant. Ps. 135:3.

Prayer does not bring God down to us, but brings us up to Him. SC 93.

The Lord direct your hearts into the love of God. 2 Thess. 3:5.

The Quote Book

No man is safe for a day or an hour without prayer. GC 530.

Wherefore let him that thinketh he standeth take heed lest he fall. 1 Cor. 10:12.

Prayer is the opening of the heart to God as to a friend. SC 93.

Pour out your heart before him. Ps. 62:8.

At the sound of fervent prayer, Satan's whole host trembles. 1T 346.

Thou believest that there is one God; thou doest well: the devils also believe, and tremble. James 2:19.

The Quote Book

The idea that prayer is not essential is one of Satan's most successful devices to ruin souls. MLT 31.

Pray, that ye enter not into temptation. Matt. 26:41.

If pride and selfishness were laid aside, five minutes would remove most difficulties. EW 119.

He that is of a proud heart stirreth up strife. Prov. 28:25.

It is impossible for any mind to comprehend all the richness and greatness of even one promise of God. TM 111.

Whereby are given unto us exceeding great and precious promises. 2 Peter 1:4.

The Quote Book

God stands back of every promise He has made. COL 147.

What he had promised, he was able also to perform. Rom. 4:21.

He who would reform others must first reform himself.
5T 614.

Thou hypocrite, first cast out the beam out of thine own eye.
Matt. 7:5.

Religion should dictate and guide you in all your pursuits, and should hold absolute control over your affections. 3T 47.

Whatsoever ye do, do all to the glory of God. 1 Cor. 10:31.

Repentance comes from Christ as truly as does pardon. DA 175.

Thou art a God ready to pardon, gracious and merciful, slow to anger, and of great kindness. Neh. 9:17.

A revival of true godliness among us is the greatest and most urgent of all our needs. 1SM 121.

What manner of persons ought ye to be in all holy conversation and godliness. 2 Peter 3:11.

A revival need be expected only in answer to prayer. 1SM 121.

These all continued with one accord in prayer and supplication. Acts 1:14.

The moment we surrender ourselves to God, believing in Him, we have His righteousness. RH 7/25/1899.

Seek ye first the kingdom of God, and his righteousness; and all these things shall be added unto you. Matt. 6:33.

The Sabbath is a golden clasp that unites God and His people. 6T 351.

Moreover also I gave them my sabbaths, to be a sign between me and them. Eze. 20:12.

Salvation is like the sunshine. It belongs to the whole world.
DA 307.

For this is good and acceptable in the sight of God our Saviour; who will have all men to be saved. 1 Tim. 2:3, 4.

Sanctification is not the work of a moment, an hour, a day, but of a lifetime. AA 560.

Of him are ye in Christ Jesus, who of God is made unto us wisdom, and righteousness, and sanctification. 1 Cor. 1:30.

God has set bounds that Satan cannot pass. Mar 64.

God is faithful, who will not suffer you to be tempted above that ye are able. 1 Cor. 10:13.

When the character of Christ shall be perfectly reproduced in His people, then He will come to claim them as His own. SD 32.

We shall also bear the image of the heavenly. 1 Cor. 15:49.

No other victory we can gain will be so precious as victory gained over self. MH 485.

Seekest thou great things for thyself? seek them not. Jer. 45:5.

In Christ we become more closely united to God than if we had never fallen. DA 25.

That they may all call upon the name of the Lord, to serve him with one consent. Zeph. 3:9.

Short sermons will be remembered far better than long ones.
GW 168.

He that shutteth his lips is esteemed a man of understanding.
Prov. 17:28.

The Quote Book

Jesus died, not to save man *in* his sins, but *from* his sins. TDG 162.

If the wicked will turn from all his sins . . . he shall surely live, he shall not die. Eze. 18:21.

Sin is an expensive business. TDG 86.

He that loveth pleasure shall be a poor man. Prov. 21:17.

The Quote Book

As soon as there was sin, there was a Saviour. IHP 13.

The living God, who is the Saviour of all men. 1 Tim. 4:10.

The Quote Book

The test of sincerity is not in words, but in deeds. TDG 244.

Is it nothing to you, all ye that pass by? Lam. 1:12.

In order to fight successfully in the battle against sin, you must keep close to Jesus. IHP 122.

Our help is in the name of the Lord. Ps. 124:8.

The Quote Book

It is ever God's purpose to bring light out of darkness, joy out of sorrow, and rest out of weariness for the waiting, longing soul. 5T 216.

Unto the upright there ariseth light in the darkness. Ps. 112:4.

The soul that has given himself to Christ is more precious in His sight than the whole world.
DA 483.

There is joy in the presence of the angels of God over one sinner that repenteth. Luke 15:10.

At the foot of the cross, remembering that for one sinner Christ would have laid down His life, you may estimate the value of a soul. COL 196.

**Herein is love, not that we loved God, but that he loved us.
1 John 4:10.**

Every soul is as fully known to Jesus as if he were the only one for whom the Saviour died.
DA 480.

Hereby perceive we the love of God, because he laid down his life for us. 1 John 3:16.

The constant burden of your hearts should be, What can I do to save souls for whom Christ died? TDG 218.

Let him know, that he which converteth the sinner . . . shall save a soul from death. James 5:20.

The Bible is the great standard of right and wrong, clearly defining sin and holiness. IHP 133.

Thy word is a lamp unto my feet, and a light unto my path. Ps. 119:105.

Our greatest strength is realized when we feel and acknowledge our weakness. 5T 70.

When I am weak, then am I strong. 2 Cor. 12:10.

There will be a people who hold so fast to the divine strength that they will be proof against every temptation. Mar 91.

**The Lord knoweth how to deliver the godly out of temptations.
2 Peter 2:9.**

The secret of success is the union of divine power with human effort. PP 509.

God . . . always causeth us to triumph in Christ. 2 Cor. 2:14.

Success depends not so much on talent as on energy and willingness. PK 219.

For if I do this thing willingly, I have a reward. 1 Cor. 9:17.

Kind words at home are blessed sunshine. SD 252.

Pleasant words are as an honeycomb, sweet to the soul, and health to the bones. Prov. 16:24.

The Quote Book

If we surrender our lives to His service, we can never be placed in a position for which God has not made provision.
COL 173.

God is with thee withersoever thou goest. Joshua 1:9.

If you are called to be a teacher, you are called to be a learner also. CPT 199.

He that teacheth man knowledge, shall not he know? Ps. 94:10.

True temperance teaches us to dispense entirely with everything hurtful and to use judiciously that which is healthful. PP 562.

Every man that striveth for the mastery is temperate in all things. 1 Cor. 9:25.

The Quote Book

If the thoughts are right, then as a result the words will be right.
TDG 66.

Out of the abundance of the heart the mouth speaketh.
Matt. 12:34.

If the thoughts are wrong, the feelings will be wrong; and the thoughts and the feelings combined make up the moral character. IHP 164.

As he thinketh in his heart, so is he. Prov. 23:7.

Our time belongs to God.
COL 342.

**Take ye heed, watch and pray: for ye know not when the time is.
Mark 13:33.**

One of the greatest evidences we have of the loving-kindness of God is His concealment of the events of the morrow. TMK 358.

Take therefore no thought for the morrow: for the morrow shall take thought for the things of itself. Matt. 6:34.

The Christian's life is not a modification or improvement of the old, but a transformation of nature. DA 172.

If any man be in Christ, he is a new creature: old things are passed away; behold, all things are become new. 2 Cor. 5:17.

The happiest people in the world are those who trust in Jesus and gladly do His bidding. IHP 262.

My heart trusted in him, and I am helped. Ps. 28:7.

Age does not make error truth, nor truth error. 6T 142.

The truth of the Lord endureth for ever. Ps. 117:2.

The Quote Book

You will never reach the truth if you study the Scriptures to vindicate your own ideas.
MYP 260.

Ever learning, and never able to come to the knowledge of the truth. 2 Tim. 3:7.

Harmony and union existing among men of varied dispositions is the strongest witness that can be borne that God has sent His Son into the world to save sinners. 8T 242.

Behold, how good and how pleasant it is for brethren to dwell together in unity! Ps. 133:1.

Nothing can happen in any part of the universe without the knowledge of Him who is omnipresent. 3BC 1141.

The eyes of the Lord are in every place, beholding the evil and the good. Prov. 15:3.

When the will is placed on the Lord's side, the Holy Spirit takes that will and makes it one with the divine will. OHC 104.

Wherefore be ye not unwise, but understanding what the will of the Lord is. Eph. 5:17.

All heaven is at the command of those who, realizing their lack of wisdom, come directly to the source of wisdom. To such ones God gives liberally and upbraids not. IHP 294.

If any of you lack wisdom, let him ask of God, that giveth to all men liberally, and upbraideth not; and it shall be given him. James 1:5.

Woman should fill the position which God originally designed for her, as her husband's equal. AH 231.

For as the woman is of the man, even so is the man also by the woman. 1 Cor. 11:12.

The Lord knew what was for man's happiness when He gave him work to do. 2T 529.

Thou shalt eat the labour of thine hands: happy shalt thou be. Ps. 128:2.

All who work for God should have the Martha and the Mary attributes blended—a willingness to minister and a sincere love of the truth. 6T 118.

Therefore . . . be ye stedfast, unmoveable, always abounding in the work of the Lord. 1 Cor. 15:58.

The Quote Book

Our little world, under the curse of sin the one dark blot in His glorious creation, will be honored above all other worlds in the universe of God. DA 26.

Who gave himself for our sins, that he might deliver us from this present evil world. Gal. 1:4.

When we really believe that God loves us and means to do us good we shall cease to worry about the future. MB 101.

Rest in the Lord, and wait patiently for him: fret not thyself. Ps. 37:7.

Nine tenths of the trials and perplexities that so many worry over are either imaginary, or brought upon themselves by their own wrong course. ST 12/17/1885.

Thou art careful and troubled about many things. Luke 10:41.

Morning and evening the heavenly universe take notice of every praying household.
CG 519.

In the morning will I direct my prayer unto thee. Ps. 5:3.